More HIDE & SPEAK FRENCH

Catherine Bruzzone and Sam Hutchinson
French text: Marie-Thérèse Bougard
Illustrated by Louise Comfort

BARRON'S

Ma maison—My house

1	Papa est dans **la cuisine**.	1	Dad is in **the kitchen**.
2	Je lis dans **le salon**.	2	I am reading in **the living room**.
3	**Ma chambre** est petite.	3	**My bedroom** is small.
4	Il y a deux **toilettes**.	4	There are two **toilets**.
5	**La salle de bain** est grande.	5	**The bathroom** is big.
6	**Le plafond** est haut.	6	**The ceiling** is high.
7	Maman descend **l'escalier**.	7	Mom is coming down **the stairs**.
8	**Le jardin** est derrière la maison.	8	**The garden** is behind the house.
9	Il y a un oiseau sur **le toit**.	9	There is a bird on **the roof**.

Les pièces de la maison—Rooms of the house

la cuisine
la kwee-zeen

le salon
leh sah-loh

la chambre
lah shambr

les toilettes
leh twah-let

la salle de bain
lah sal-deh-bah

le plafond
leh plaf-on

l'escalier
less-kalee-eh

le jardin
leh shar-dah

le toit
leh twah

Pendant la semaine—During the week

1 **Lundi**, je vais à l'école.	1 On **Monday**, I go to school.
2 **Mardi**, je fais de la natation.	2 On **Tuesday**, I go swimming.
3 **Mercredi**, je vais au cinéma.	3 On **Wednesday**, I go to the movies.
4 **Jeudi**, je joue au foot.	4 On **Thursday**, I play soccer.
5 **Vendredi**, je regarde la télé.	5 On **Friday**, I watch television.
6 **Samedi**, je vais chez mon ami.	6 On **Saturday**, I go to my friend's house.
7 **Dimanche**, je visite ma grand-mère.	7 On **Sunday**, I visit my grandma.
8 **Aujourd'hui**, je prépare le dîner.	8 **Today**, I am cooking supper.
9 **Demain**, je vais à une fête.	9 **Tomorrow**, I am going to a party.

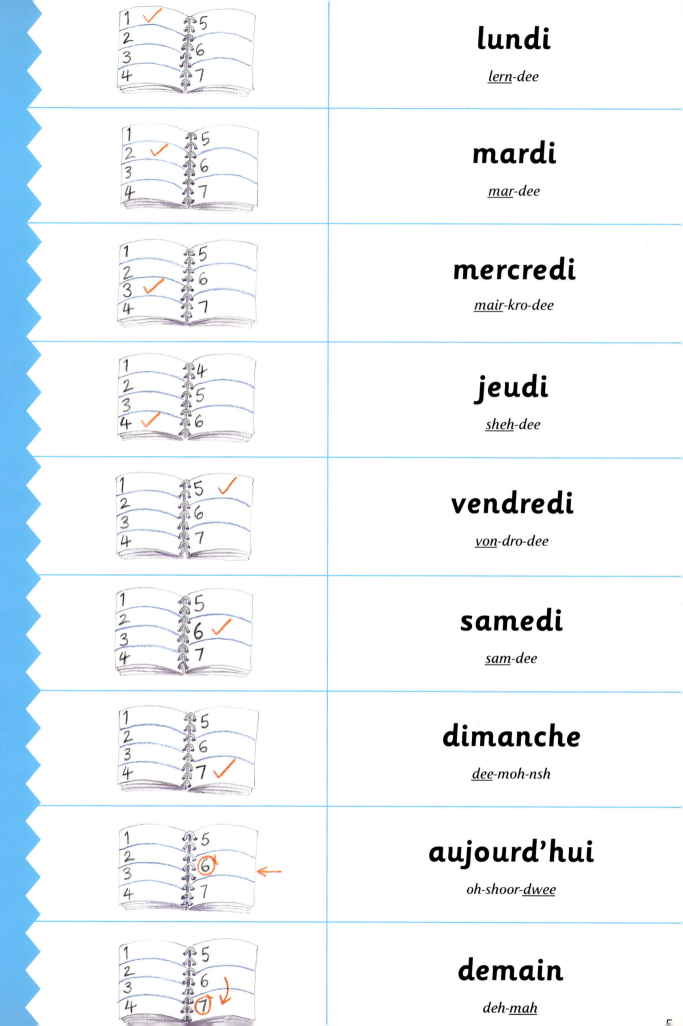

lundi

lern-dee

mardi

mar-dee

mercredi

mair-kro-dee

jeudi

sheh-dee

vendredi

von-dro-dee

samedi

sam-dee

dimanche

dee-moh-nsh

aujourd'hui

oh-shoor-dwee

demain

deh-mah

Visiter un ami—Visiting a friend

1 **Bonjour**, Marie. Entre.	1 **Hello**, Mary. Come in.
2 **Oui**, j'aime ce jeu d'ordinateur.	2 **Yes**, I like this computer game.
3 **Non**, je n'aime pas ce CD.	3 **No**, I don't like this CD.
4 Je peux avoir quelque chose à boire, **s'il vous plaît**?	4 Can I have a drink, **please**?
5 **Voilà**. Attention!	5 **Here you are**. Be careful!
6 Oups, **pardon**!	6 Oops, **sorry**!
7 **Ça va**. Ne t'inquiète pas.	7 **That's okay**. Don't worry.
8 **Au revoir**, reviens demain.	8 **Good-bye**, come again tomorrow.
9 **Merci**. À demain!	9 **Thanks**. See you tomorrow!

bonjour

boh-shoor

oui

wee

non

noh

s'il vous plaît

seel-voo-pleh

voilà

vwah-lah

pardon

par-doh

ça va

sah-vah

au revoir

oh-ro-vwah

merci

mair-see

Au parc—At the park

1	**La fille** est sur **la balançoire**.	1	**The girl** is on **the swing**.
2	Guillaume et Annie sont sur **la bascule**.	2	William and Annie are on **the seesaw**.
3	Il y a un chien dans **l'allée**.	3	There is a dog on **the path**.
4	**Le garçon** tient **le cerf-volant**.	4	**The boy** is holding **the kite**.
5	Le cygne nage sur **le lac**.	5	The swan is swimming on **the lake**.
6	Maman est sur **le banc**.	6	Mom is on **the bench**.
7	**L'enfant** court vers sa maman.	7	**The child** is running toward his mom.

la fille

lah fee

la balançoire

lah balon-swah

la bascule

lah bask-yool

l'allée

lal-eh

le garçon

leh gar-soh

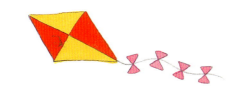

le cerf-volant

leh sair-voloh

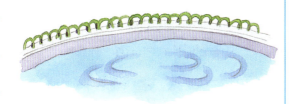

le lac

leh lack

le banc

leh bonk

l'enfant

lon-foh

Jouons!—Let's play!

1	Les équipes jouent au **football**.	1	The teams are playing **soccer**.
2	Mes amis jouent au **ping-pong**.	2	My friends are playing **table tennis**.
3	Mon père aime **faire du ski**.	3	My father likes **skiing**.
4	Mon frère **pêche** dans le lac.	4	My brother **is fishing** in the lake.
5	Ma sœur est bonne en **gymnastique**.	5	My sister is good at **gymnastics**.
6	Marc est bon en **athlétisme**.	6	Mark is good at **athletics**.
7	Ma mère **fait du vélo**.	7	My mother **is riding a bike**.
8	Je **nage** tous les jours.	8	I **swim** every day.
9	Les garçons jouent au **basket**.	9	The boys are playing **basketball**.

le football

leh foot<u>bol</u>

le ping-pong

leh peeng-<u>pong</u>

faire du ski

fair-doo-<u>skee</u>

la pêche

lah pesh

la gymnastique

lah jeem-nass-<u>teek</u>

l'athlétisme

lat-leh-<u>tees</u>-m

faire du vélo

fair doo <u>vay</u>-loh

nager

nah-<u>shay</u>

le basket

leh bas<u>ket</u>

En ville—In town

1 **L'école** a un toit marron.	1 **The school** has a brown roof.
2 Il y a **une maison** blanche au coin de la rue.	2 There is **a** white **house** on the corner of the street.
3 Le train quitte **la gare**.	3 The train is leaving **the station**.
4 **La poste** est derrière **le supermarché**.	4 **The post office** is behind **the supermarket**.
5 Il y a beaucoup de **magasins**.	5 There are lots of **stores**.
6 **L'usine** est très grande.	6 **The factory** is very big.
7 Il y a la queue au **cinéma**.	7 There is a line at **the movies**.
8 **Le marché** est plein de monde.	8 **The market** is very busy.

La ville—The town

l'école
leh-<u>kol</u>

la maison
lah may-<u>zoh</u>

la gare
lah gaar

la poste
lah post

le supermarché
leh soo-pair-marsh-<u>eh</u>

le magasin
leh mag-ah-<u>zah</u>

l'usine
loo-<u>zeen</u>

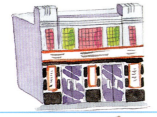

le cinéma
leh see-nay-<u>mah</u>

le marché
leh mar-<u>shay</u>

Au supermarché—At the supermarket

1	Il n'y a pas de **pain**!	1	There's no **bread**!
2	**Les œufs** sont cassés.	2	**The eggs** are broken.
3	Le chien vole **la viande**.	3	The dog is stealing **the meat**.
4	L'homme coupe **le poisson**.	4	The man is cutting **the fish**.
5	**Le riz** est à côté **des pâtes**.	5	**The rice** is next to **the pasta**.
6	**Le beurre** est très cher.	6	**The butter** is very expensive.
7	Le chat boit **le lait**.	7	The cat is drinking **the milk**.
8	Maman achète du **sucre**.	8	Mom is buying **sugar**.

le pain

leh pah

l'œuf

luhf

la viande

lah vee-ond

le poisson

leh pwah-son

le riz

leh ree

les pâtes

leh pat

le beurre

leh ber

le lait

leh lay

le sucre

leh syoo-kro

Acheter des fruits—Buying fruit

1	**Les pommes** sont vertes.	1	**The apples** are green.
2	La femme mange **une pêche**.	2	The woman is eating **a peach**.
3	Il y a beaucoup de **cerises**.	3	There are lots of **cherries**.
4	**Les oranges** sont juteuses.	4	**The oranges** are juicy.
5	**L'ananas** est énorme!	5	**The pineapple** is huge!
6	**Les mangues** sont délicieuses.	6	**The mangoes** are delicious.
7	L'enfant lance **la banane**.	7	The child is throwing **the banana**.
8	L'oiseau veut **les raisins**.	8	The bird wants **the grapes**.
9	**Les fraises** sont rouges.	9	**The strawberries** are red.

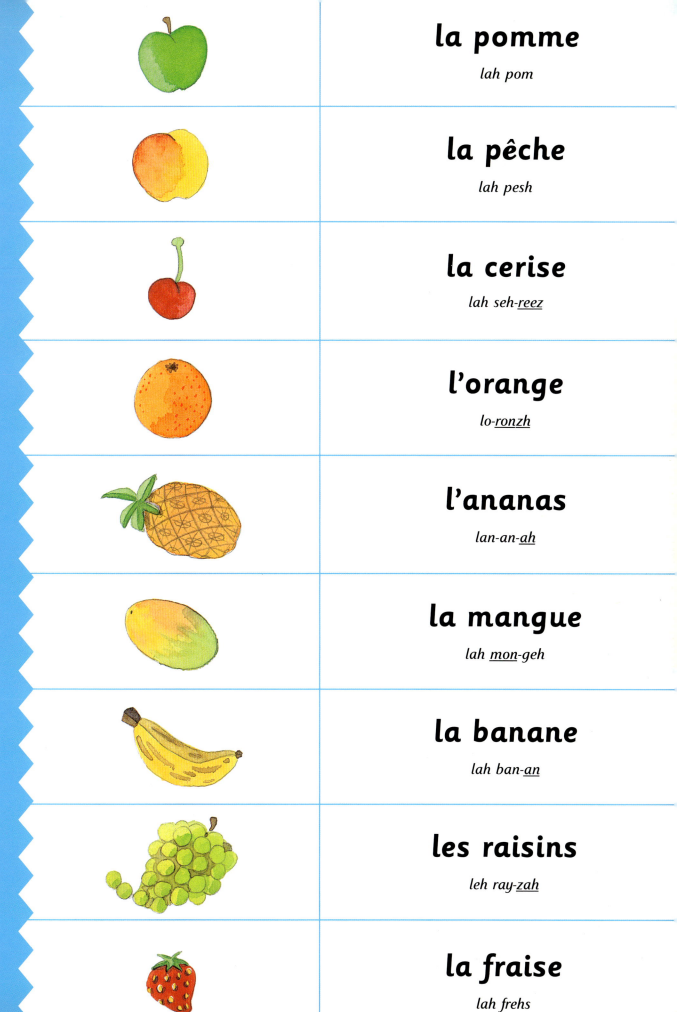

la pomme
lah pom

la pêche
lah pesh

la cerise
lah seh-reez

l'orange
lo-ronzh

l'ananas
lan-an-ah

la mangue
lah mon-geh

la banane
lah ban-an

les raisins
leh ray-zah

la fraise
lah frehs

Acheter des vêtements—Shopping for clothes

1	Le chapeau est trop **grand**.	1	The hat is too **big**.
2	La robe est trop **petite**.	2	The dress is too **small**.
3	L'écharpe est trop **longue**.	3	The scarf is too **long**.
4	Le pantalon est trop **court**.	4	The pants are too **short**.
5	Le manteau est **cher**.	5	The coat is **expensive**.
6	La robe est **jolie**.	6	The dress is **pretty**.
7	La petite fille est **heureuse**.	7	The little girl is **happy**.
8	Le petit garçon est **triste**.	8	The little boy is **sad**.
9	La glace est **bonne**.	9	The ice cream is **good**.

grand/grande

groh/grond

petit/petite

puh-tee/puh-teet

long/longue

loh/lon-geh

court/courte

kor/kort

cher/chère

share/share

joli/jolie

zhol-ee/zhol-ee

heureux/heureuse

eh-ruh/eh-ruhz

triste

treest

bon/bonne

boh/bon

Quel temps fait-il?—What's the weather?

1 **Le soleil** brille à la plage.

2 **Il fait chaud**.

3 Mais **il pleut** sur la colline.

4 Et **les nuages** sont gris.

5 Et **le vent** est fort.

6 Il y a **un orage** magnifique!

7 Sur la mer il y a du **brouillard**.

8 Dans les montagnes **il fait froid** et **il neige**!

1 **The sun** is shining at the beach.

2 **It's hot**.

3 But **it's raining** on the hill.

4 And **the clouds** are gray.

5 And **the wind** is strong.

6 There is **a** magnificent **storm**!

7 On the sea there is **fog**.

8 In the mountains **it's cold** and **it's snowing**!

le soleil

leh sol-ay

il fait chaud

eel fah show

il pleut

eel pluh

le nuage

leh noo-ah-sh

le vent

leh voh

l'orage

lor-ah-zh

le brouillard

leh brwee-ar

il fait froid

eel fah frwah

il neige

eel ehzh-sh

L'année (1)—The year (1)

1	Il y a quatre **saisons**.
2	J'aime **le printemps**.
3	En **mars** il y a du vent.
4	Il pleut souvent en **avril**.
5	Il y a beaucoup de fleurs en **mai**.
6	**L'été**, je vais en vacances.
7	La fleur de **juin**, c'est la rose.
8	L'anniversaire de mon ami est en **juillet**.
9	Il fait chaud en **août**.

1	There are four **seasons**.
2	I like **spring**.
3	**March** is windy.
4	It often rains in **April**.
5	There are lots of flowers in **May**.
6	In the **summer**, I go on vacation.
7	**June**'s flower is the rose.
8	My friend's birthday is in **July**.
9	It's hot in **August**.

	**la saison** *lah say-<u>zohn</u>*
	**le printemps** *leh pran-<u>tohn</u>*
	mars *marss*
	**avril** *av-<u>reel</u>*
	**mai** *may*
	**l'été** *leh-<u>tay</u>*
	**juin** *zh-<u>wah</u>*
	juillet *<u>zhwee</u>-ay*
	**août** *oot*

23

L'année (2)—The year (2)

1	**L'automne** commence en **septembre**.	1	**Fall** starts in **September**.
2	En **octobre**, les feuilles tombent.	2	In **October** the leaves fall.
3	En Australie, il fait chaud en **novembre**.	3	In Australia, it's hot in **November**.
4	En **décembre**, il y a Noël!	4	Christmas is in **December**!
5	**L'hiver** amène de la neige!	5	**Winter** brings snow.
6	En **janvier**, il fait froid.	6	It is cold in **January**.
7	Je suis allé à un carnaval en **février**.	7	I went to a carnival in **February**.
8	Il y a douze **mois** dans l'année.	8	There are twelve **months** in the year.

	l'automne *loh-ton*
9	**septembre** *sep-tom-bruh*
10	**octobre** *ok-toh-bruh*
11	**novembre** *no-vom-bruh*
	l'hiver *lee-vair*
12	**décembre** *deh-som-bruh*
1	**janvier** *zhon-vee-ay*
2	**février** *feh-vree-ay*
	le mois *leh mwah*

Cultiver des légumes—Growing vegetables

1. Il y a huit **pommes de terre**.
2. **Le maïs** est jaune.
3. **Les carottes** ont des feuilles vertes.
4. **Les choux** sont ronds.
5. **Les courgettes** et **les aubergines** sont grosses.
6. **Les tomates** et **le céleri** sont dans le panier.
7. Les bestioles mangent **les laitues**.

1. There are eight **potatoes**.
2. **The corn** is yellow.
3. **The carrots** have green leaves.
4. **The cabbages** are round.
5. **The squash** and **the eggplants** are big.
6. **The tomatoes** and **the celery** are in the basket.
7. The worms are eating **the lettuce**.

Les légumes—Vegetables

la pomme de terre

lah pom duh <u>tair</u>

le maïs

leh my-<u>eess</u>

la carotte

lah kah-<u>rot</u>

le chou

leh shoo

la courgette

lah kor-<u>shet</u>

l'aubergine

loh-bair-<u>zheen</u>

la tomate

lah to-<u>mat</u>

la laitue

lah layt-<u>yoo</u>

le céleri

leh sel-air-<u>ee</u>

Dans le forêt—In the forest

1 **Le renard** a une longue queue.

2 **L'écureuil** est sur la branche.

3 **Le cerf** mange des feuilles.

4 Où est **l'ours** brun?

5 **Le lapin** court vers son terrier.

6 Il y a beaucoup de **papillons**.

7 **Les scarabées** sont noirs.

8 **La chenille** est sur la feuille.

9 **Les mouches** sont énervantes!

1 **The fox** has a long tail.

2 **The squirrel** is on the branch.

3 **The deer** is eating the leaves.

4 Where is **the** brown **bear**?

5 **The rabbit** runs into its burrow.

6 There are lots of **butterflies**.

7 **The beetles** are black.

8 **The caterpillar** is on the leaf.

9 **The flies** are annoying!

le renard
leh ruhn-<u>ar</u>

l'écureuil
leh-koo-<u>reh</u>-ee

le cerf
leh sairf

l'ours
loorss

le lapin
leh lah-<u>pah</u>

le papillon
leh papee-<u>ohn</u>

le scarabée
leh skah-rah-<u>bay</u>

la chenille
lah sher-<u>nee</u>-yeh

la mouche
lah moosh

Questions—Questions

1 **Qui** est cet homme?	1 **Who** is that man?
2 **Qu'est-ce que** c'est?	2 **What**'s that?
3 **Quand** est-ce que vous fermez?	3 **When** do you close?
4 **Où** sont mes lunettes?	4 **Where** are my glasses?
5 **Pourquoi** rit-il?	5 **Why** is he laughing?
6 **Comment** dit-on "chien"?	6 **How** do you say "dog"?
7 Ça coûte **combien**?	7 **How much** does this cost?
8 Il a **combien** d'animaux?	8 **How many** animals does he have
9 **Je peux** vous aider?	9 **Can I** help you?

qui?

kee

qu'est-ce que?

kess-kuh

quand?

kohn

où?

ooh

pourquoi?

poor-kwah

comment?

kom-ohn

combien? **(how much)**

kom-bee-ehn

combien? **(how many)**

kom-bee-ehn

puis-je?

pwee-zh

Word List

Ma maison p. 2 — My house
Les pièces de la maison — Rooms of the house

la chambre	bedroom
la cuisine	kitchen
l'escalier	stairs
le jardin	garden
le plafond	ceiling
la salle de bain	bathroom
le salon	living room
les toilettes	toilet
le toit	roof

Pendant la semaine p. 4 — During the week
Les jours de la semaine — Days of the week

lundi	Monday
mardi	Tuesday
mercredi	Wednesday
jeudi	Thursday
vendredi	Friday
samedi	Saturday
dimanche	Sunday
aujourd'hui	today
demain	tomorrow

Visiter un ami p. 6 — Visiting a friend
Expressions utiles — Useful expressions

au revoir	good-bye
bonjour	hello
ça va	that's okay
merci	thanks
non	no
oui	yes
pardon	sorry
s'il vous plaît	please
voilà	there you are

Au parc p. 8 — At the park
Le parc — The park

l'allée	path
la balançoire	swing
le banc	bench
la bascule	seesaw
le cerf-volant	kite
l'enfant	child
la fille	girl
le garçon	boy
le lac	lake

Jouons! p. 10 — Let's play!
Le sport — Sports

l'athlétisme	athletics
le basket	basketball
faire du ski	skiing
faire du vélo	riding a bike
le football	soccer
la gymnastique	gymnastics
nager	swimming
la pêche	fishing
le ping-pong	table tennis

En ville p.12 — In town
La ville — The town

le cinéma	movies
l'école	school
la gare	station
le magasin	store
la maison	house
le marché	market
la poste	post office
le supermarché	supermarket
l'usine	factory

Au supermarché p.14 — At the supermarket
Le supermarché — The supermarket

le beurre	butter
le lait	milk
l'œuf	egg
le pain	bread
les pâtes	pasta
le poisson	fish
le riz	rice
le sucre	sugar
la viande	meat

Acheter des fruits p.16 — Buying fruit
Les fruits — Fruit

l'ananas	pineapple
la banane	banana
la cerise	cherry
la fraise	strawberry
la mangue	mango
l'orange	orange
la pêche	peach
la pomme	apple
les raisins	grapes

Acheter des vêtements p.18 — Shopping for clothes
Les adjectifs — Adjectives

joli/jolie	pretty
bon/bonne	good
cher/chère	expensive
court/courte	short
grand/grande	big
heureux/heureuse	happy
long/longue	long
petit/petite	small
triste	sad

Quel temps fait-il? p.20 — What's the weather?
Le temps — Weather

le brouillard	fog
il fait chaud	it's hot
il fait froid	it's cold
il neige	it's snowing
le nuage	cloud
l'orage	storm
il pleut	it's raining
le soleil	sun
le vent	wind

L'année (1) p.22 — The year (1)
Le printemps et l'été — Spring and summer

la saison	season
le printemps	spring
mars	March
avril	April
mai	May
l'été	summer
juin	June
juillet	July
août	August

L'année (2) p.24 — The year (2)
L'automne et l'hiver — Fall and winter

l'automne	fall
septembre	September
octobre	October
novembre	November
l'hiver	winter
décembre	December
janvier	January
février	February
le mois	month

Cultiver des légumes p.26 — Growing vegetables
Les légumes — Vegetables

l'aubergine	eggplant
la carotte	carrot
le céleri	celery
le chou	cabbage
la courgette	squash
la laitue	lettuce
le maïs	corn
la pomme de terre	potato
la tomate	tomato

Dans la forêt p.28 — In the forest
Les animaux et les insectes — Animals and insects

le cerf	deer
la chenille	caterpillar
l'écureuil	squirrel
le lapin	rabbit
la mouche	fly
l'ours brun	brown bear
le papillon	butterfly
le renard	fox
le scarabée	beetle

Questions p.30 — Questions
Questions — Questions

combien?	how many?
combien?	how much?
comment?	how?
où?	where?
pourquoi?	why?
je peux?	can I?
quand?	when?
qu'est-ce que?	what?
qui?	who?